Welcome to the
'Highly Tooned World'
of
Rallying

The Rallyist

Cartoons by

Paul M. Ellender

Rallyist
Publications

A Rallyist Publication

First Edition: Launched June 2009
Published by Rallyist Publications
Produced & Edited by Paul M. Ellender

ISBN 978-0-9562214-0-7

Printed by
Mixam Uk Ltd
Watford
ENGLAND

Rallyist Publications.
Leyland
Lancashire
United Kingdom

Th'Artist

Apparently, I can't draw Horses, unlike my Father or my Uncle Vic. Not my fault, it's just I've never felt the need. Not that I've anything against Horses you understand, my interest has always focused on Horsepower. A former Formula Ford 1600, Vauxhall Chevette and Alfasud Prod-Saloon Racing Driver, I have always fostered a passion for motor sport.

My connection to Rallying however came not from the curious Racing Lines I could adopt navigating a route through the corners of the Racing Circuits of Britain, or even my ability to still control the car when driving next to the track rather than on it. My association came via membership with The Clitheroe and District Motor Club, participating as Event and Sector Marshall. This activity introduced me to the people and characters of the Rallying world and ultimately the humour. From this, the humour was soon converted into cartoon form for the then Club Newsletter 'Wrongslot'.

Over the Years that followed the Style and Artwork was honed and polished until the Rallyist was truly born finally finding support from British Rally Championship with inclusion in their Programmes.

Now they are available for everyone.

Paul McEllereda

To
Frank Havard

For
Starting this
Whole Rally Cartoon Thing Off

My Thanks

Sadly it was one of the lesser known
Casualties of the Group B Ban.

And I'm supposed to trust you with my £30,000 Highly Tuned Precision Built Machine?

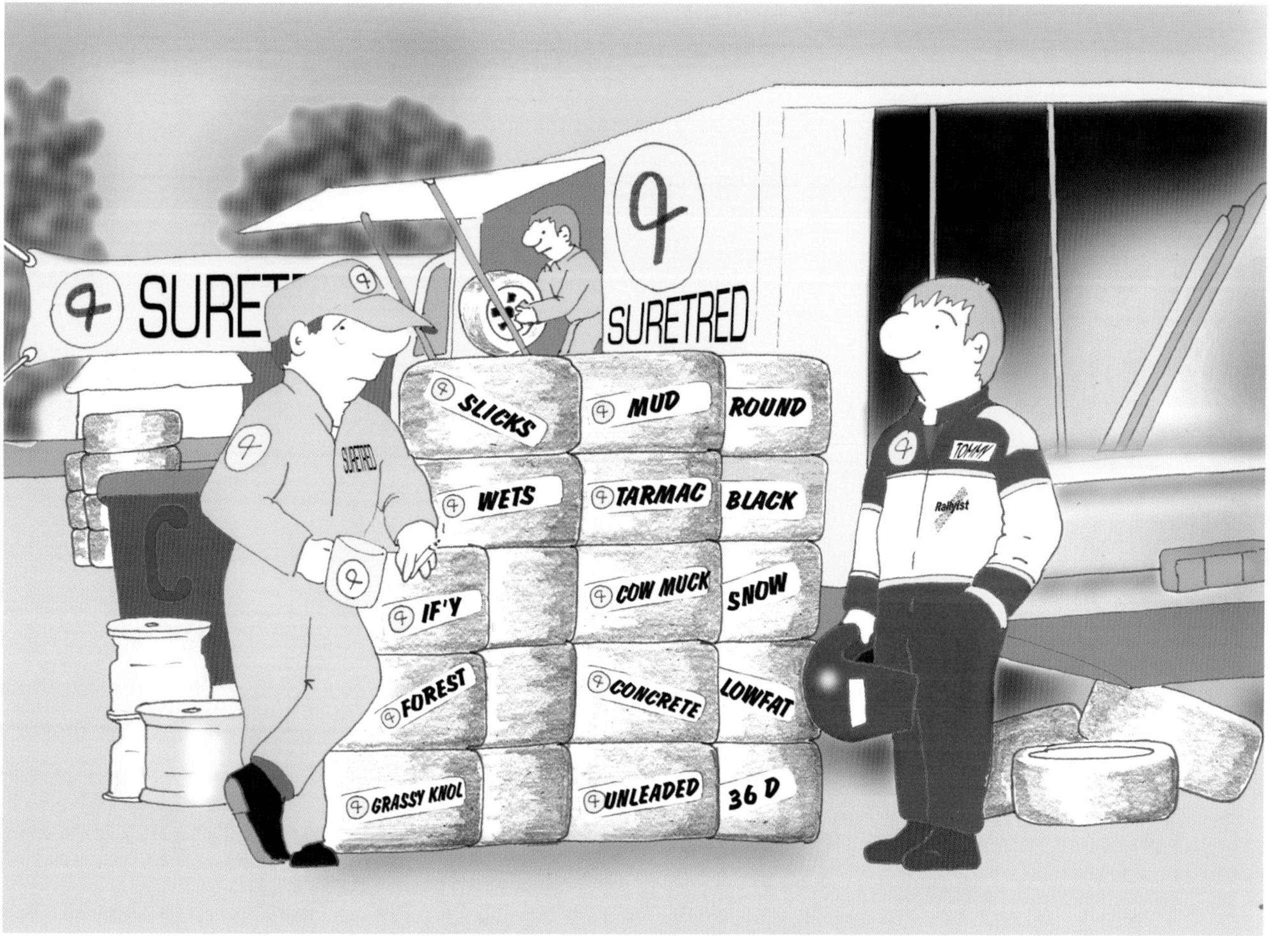
SURETRED
SLICKS
MUD
ROUND
WETS
TARMAC
BLACK
IF'Y
COW MUCK
SNOW
FOREST
CONCRETE
LOWFAT
GRASSY KNOL
UNLEADED
36 D
TOMMY
Rallyist

Which are Cheapest?

I think we may have spotted a problem with the tyre idea...

Ted Lad, I don't care if your Mum has put her washing out or if you did hear a Blackbird sing. What Tyres do I use?

Look Bill, I know we are on a low budget
but do you think I could have a seat?

And that was only the third
car to go through!

How was I going to know it was the last
episode of the series tonight?

Are you sure its the
Manx Rally this week?

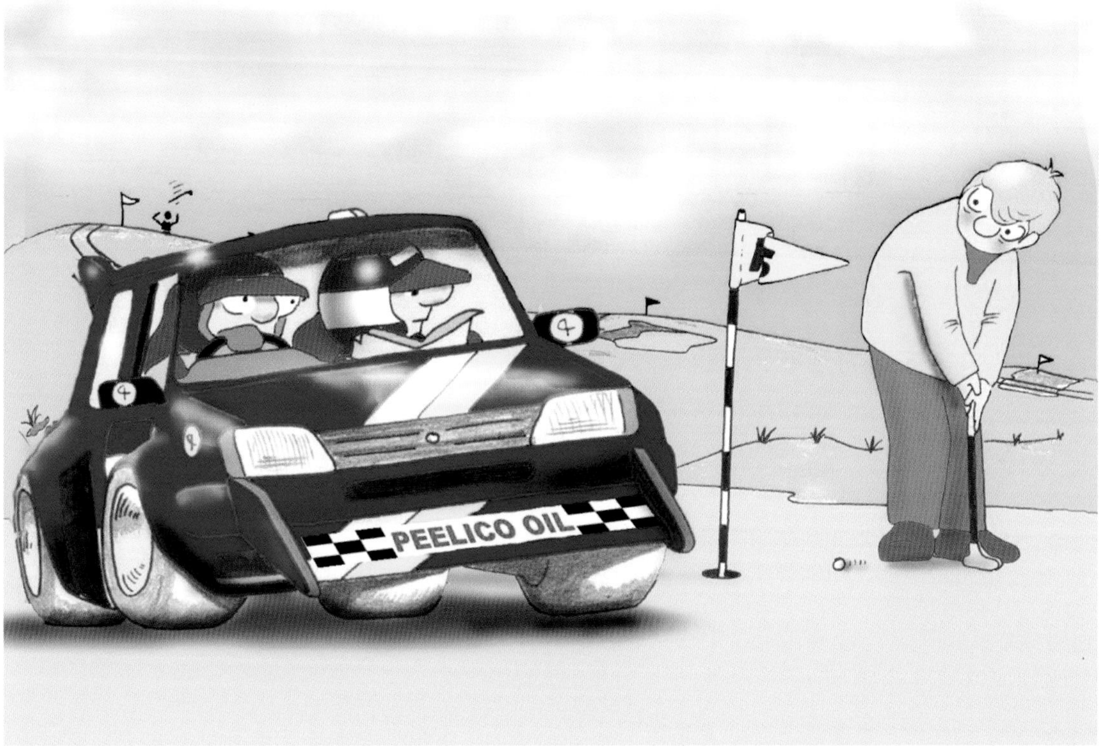
PEELICO OIL

Paul M Ellerd

Its OK, he's waiting for the little
finger to go round again.

16

Well worth the effort, Pet!
Just look at that View..
Bet your glad you came now?

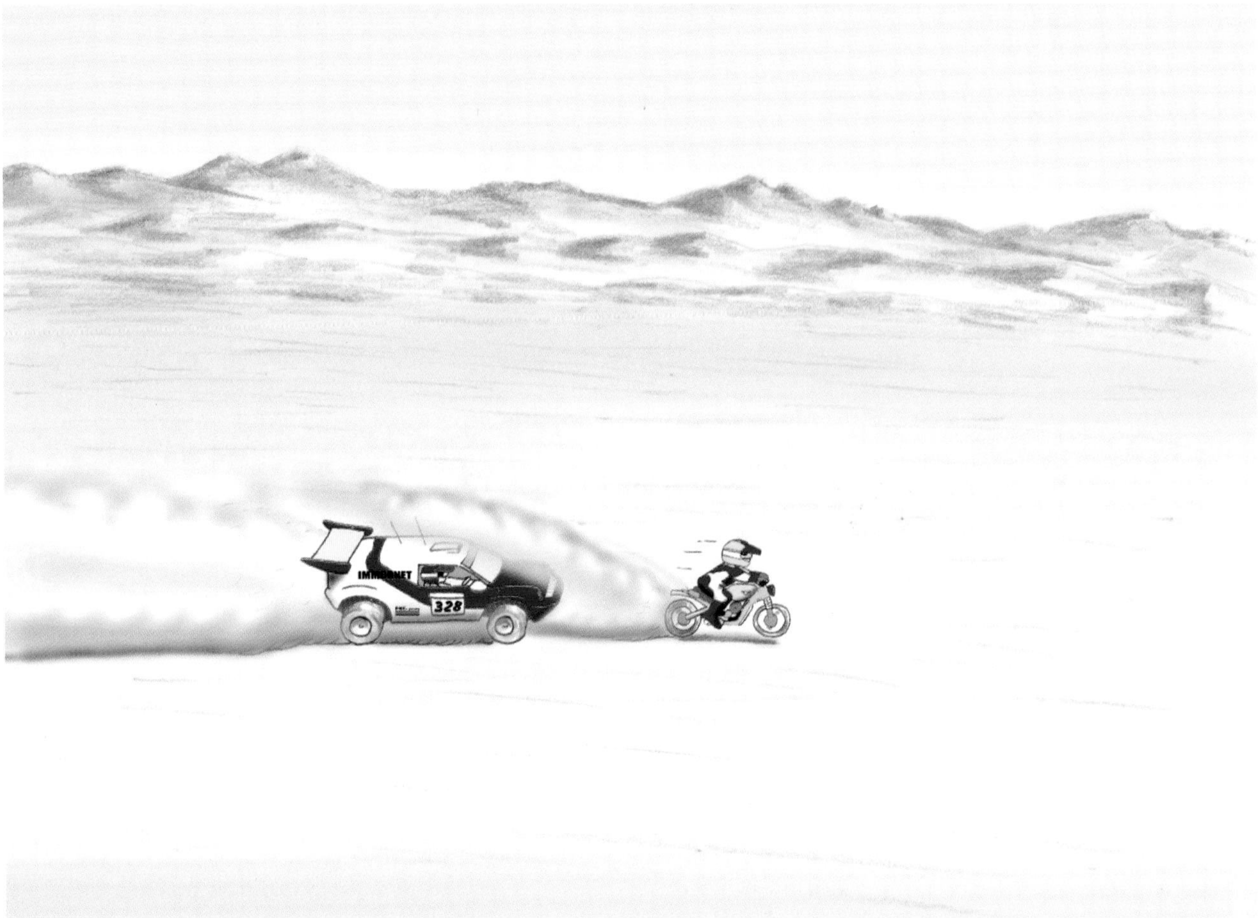
328

MOVE OVER!!!!

Said we should have tested it first!

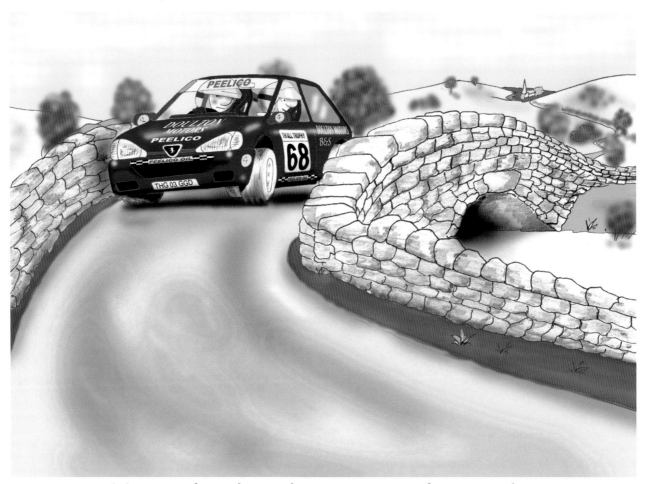

Hey, they've done a cracking job
repairing last years....little error?

20

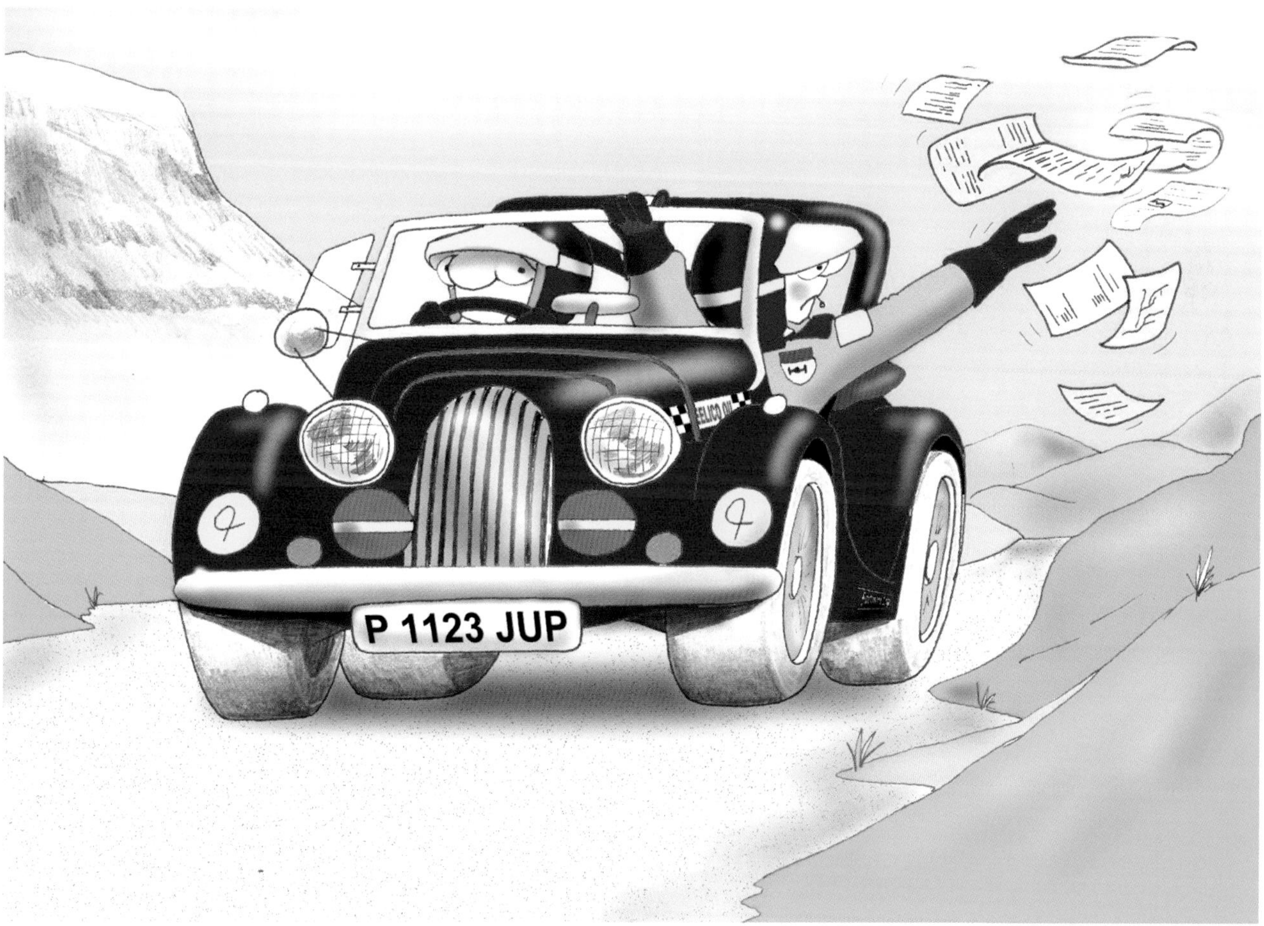
P 1123 JUP

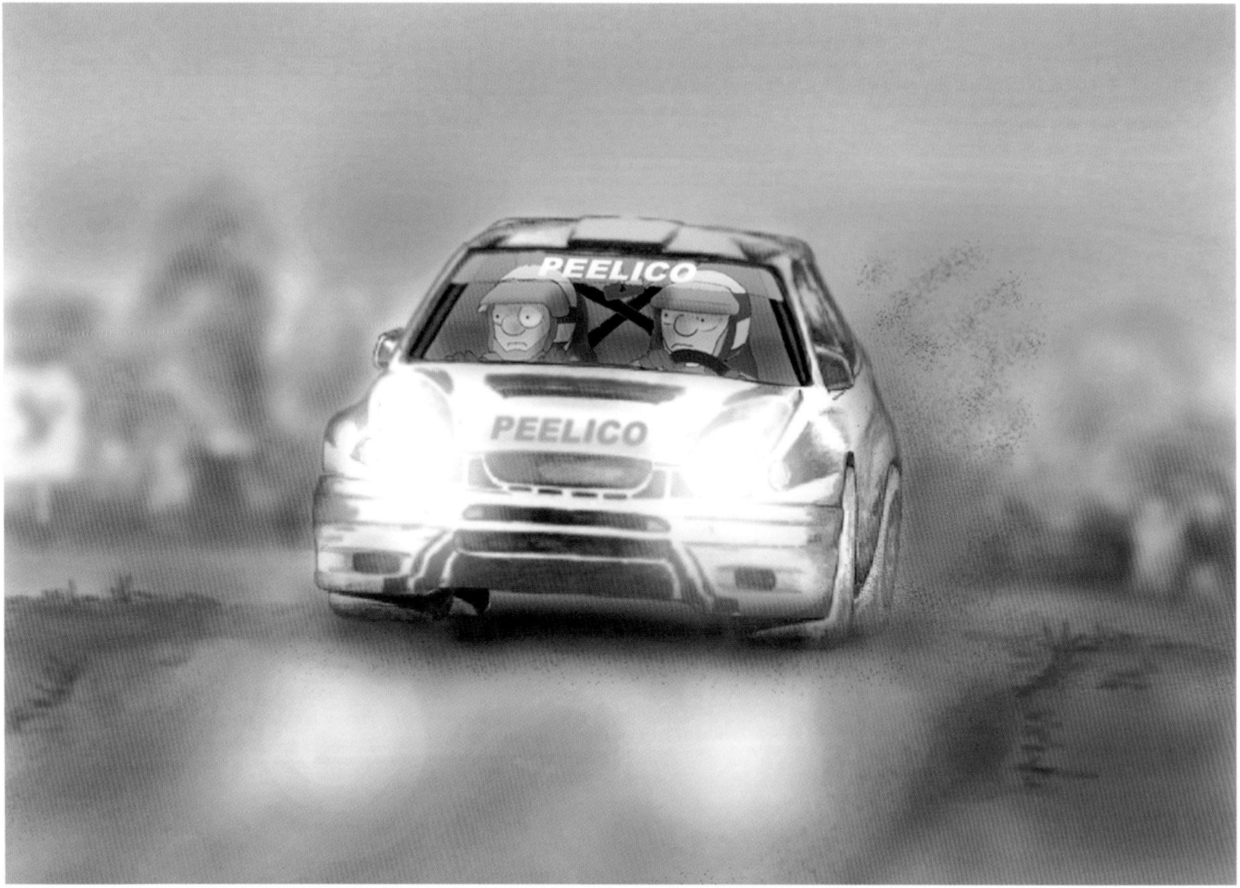
PEELICO
PEELICO

Caution..Slippy left 2...Woe Very Slippy
Right 3...Fairly Fast, but don't be silly,
Slippy left 4 drop...

Paul Mc Ellenel

I notice you gave yourself plenty of room
going through that Gate!

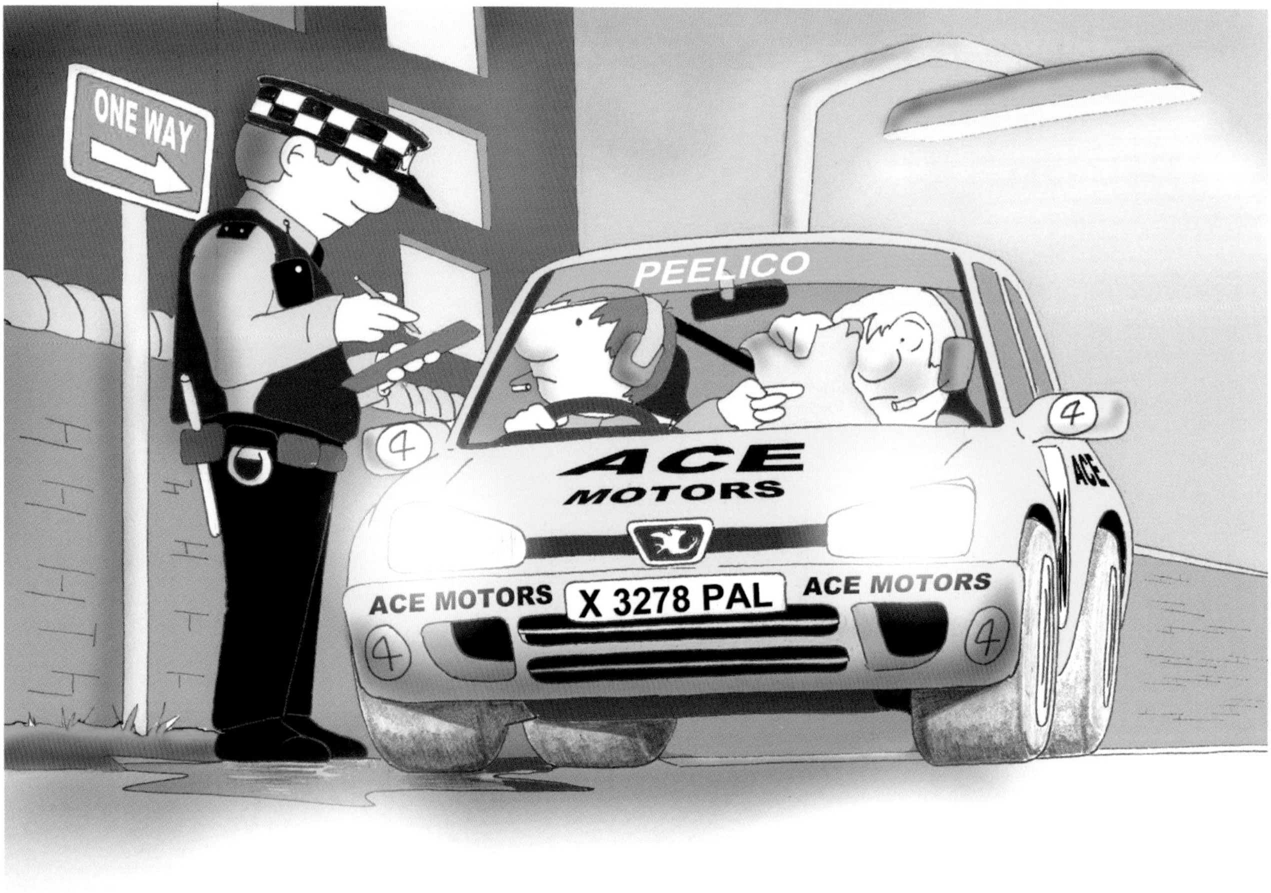
ONE WAY
PEELICO
ACE
MOTORS
ACE
ACE MOTORS
X 3278 PAL
ACE MOTORS
4
4
4
4

He Told Me Too!

Paul M Ellerd

God this Car is Bloody uncomfortable!

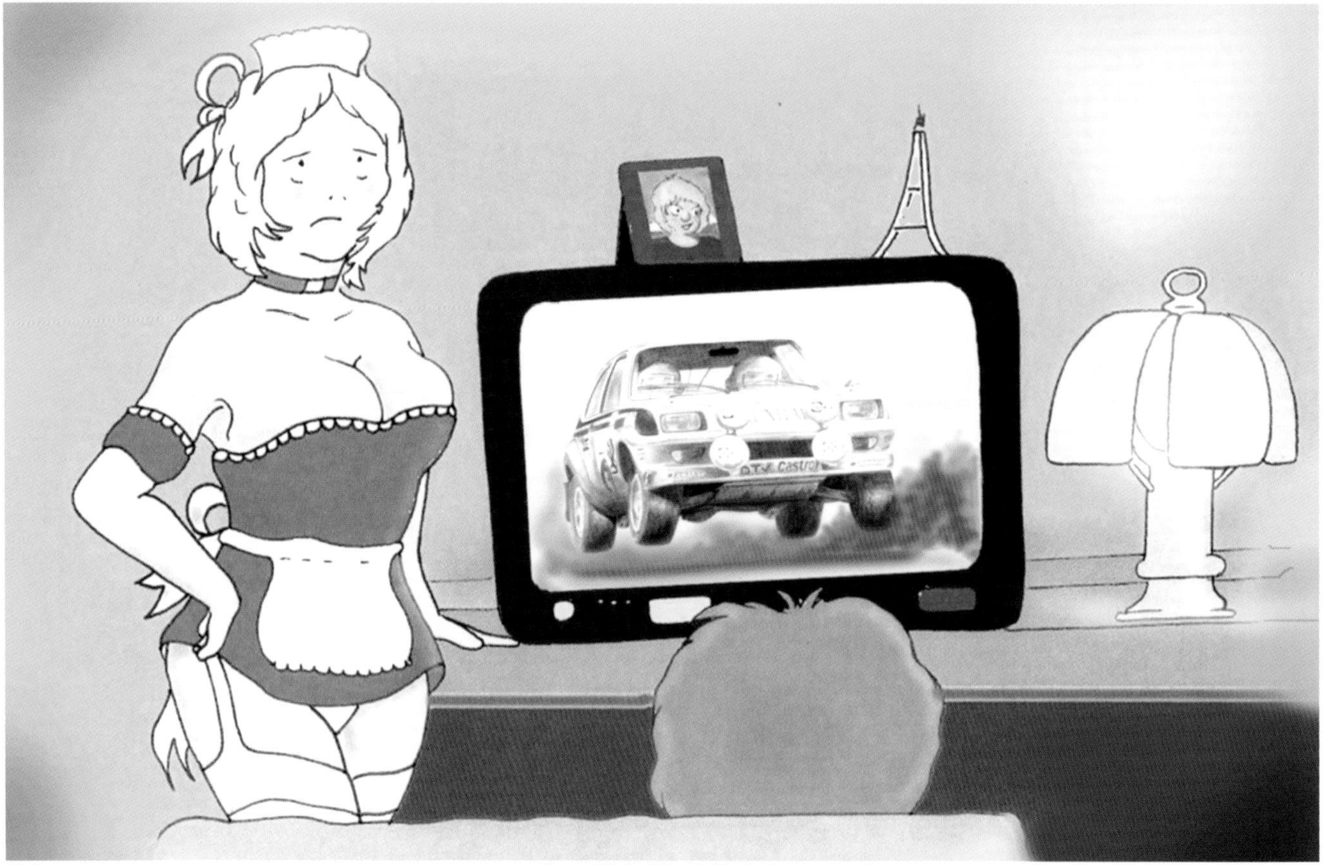

Put Kettle on Pet.

How can you possibly be 'Airsick'
in a car?

All I said was, I would have thought
we may have needed slightly more detail than
that of your Daily Xpress Map of the World!

I think we may have a spot
of Damp in the electrics!

Nothing beats a nice drive
in the country. If you spot a nice Pub..

Right 3 100 into left 2 caution gate, 200 left 3
.....pick up cat food and pay for the paper's?

You couldn't do that after you've
seen to us?

Half way through a Stage
and you want me to Stop to look at something!

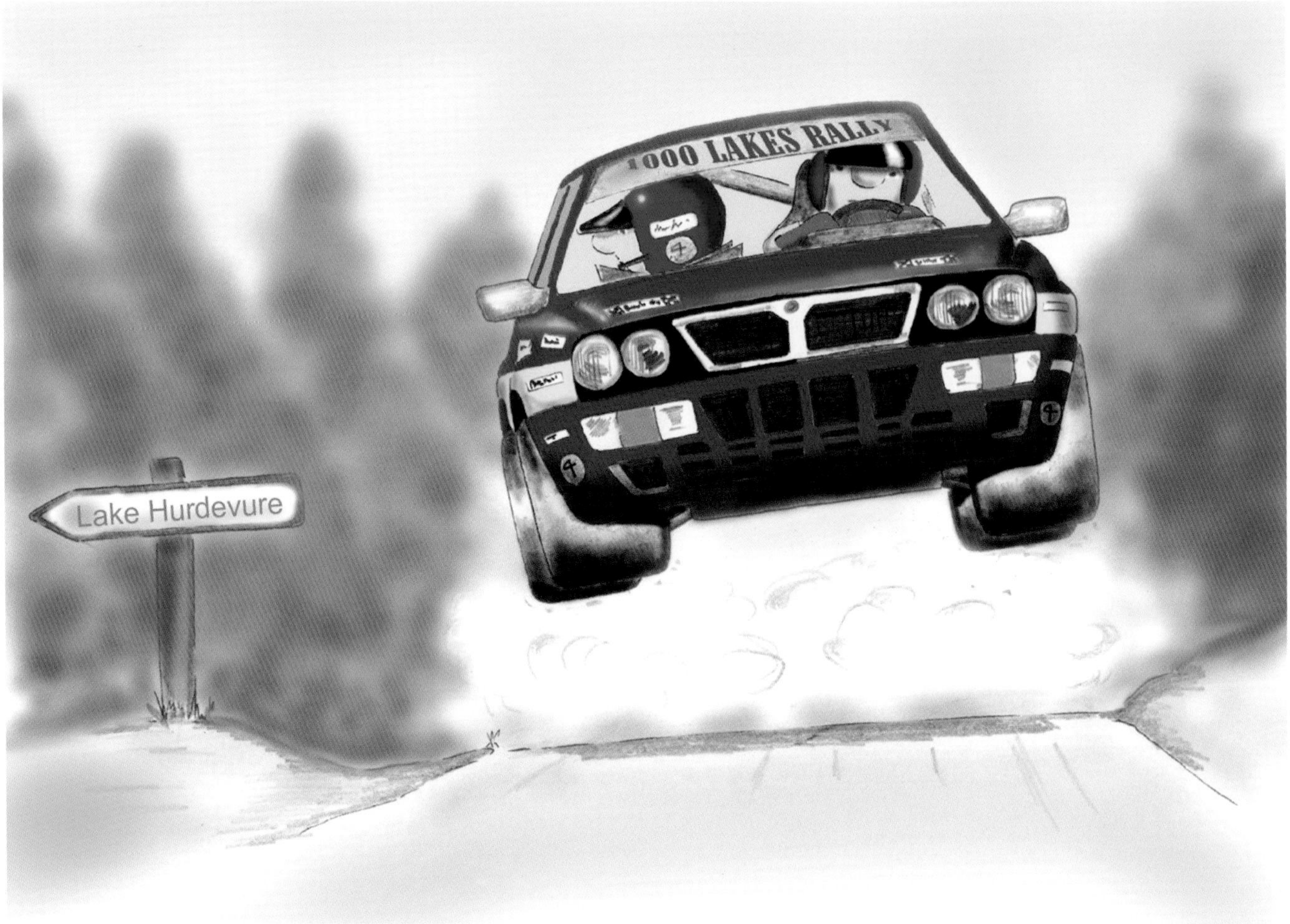
1000 LAKES RALLY
Lake Hurdevure

.............231........

Paul M Ellenl

We are car number 32
and you can't see whats wrong!

Honestly, You were only complaining the other day
that I never take you out.

Something extra in my Drink
What makes you think that?

And that Sir, is what I call
a Flying Finish!

You know sometimes I can see the attraction
of being a Golf Widow.

A bit of a pain, the whole
service crew getting that bug at the same time, eh?

You know this cars handling terrible
since we got hauled out of that ditch...

Well whose jobs was it to bring the Car?

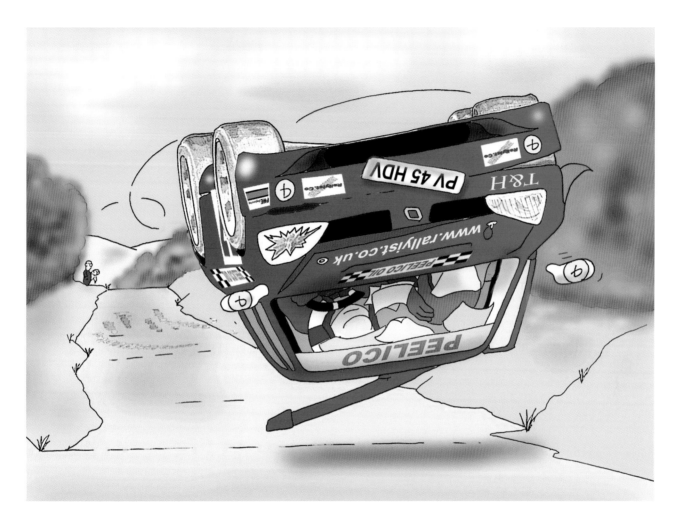

I hope someones Videoing this.

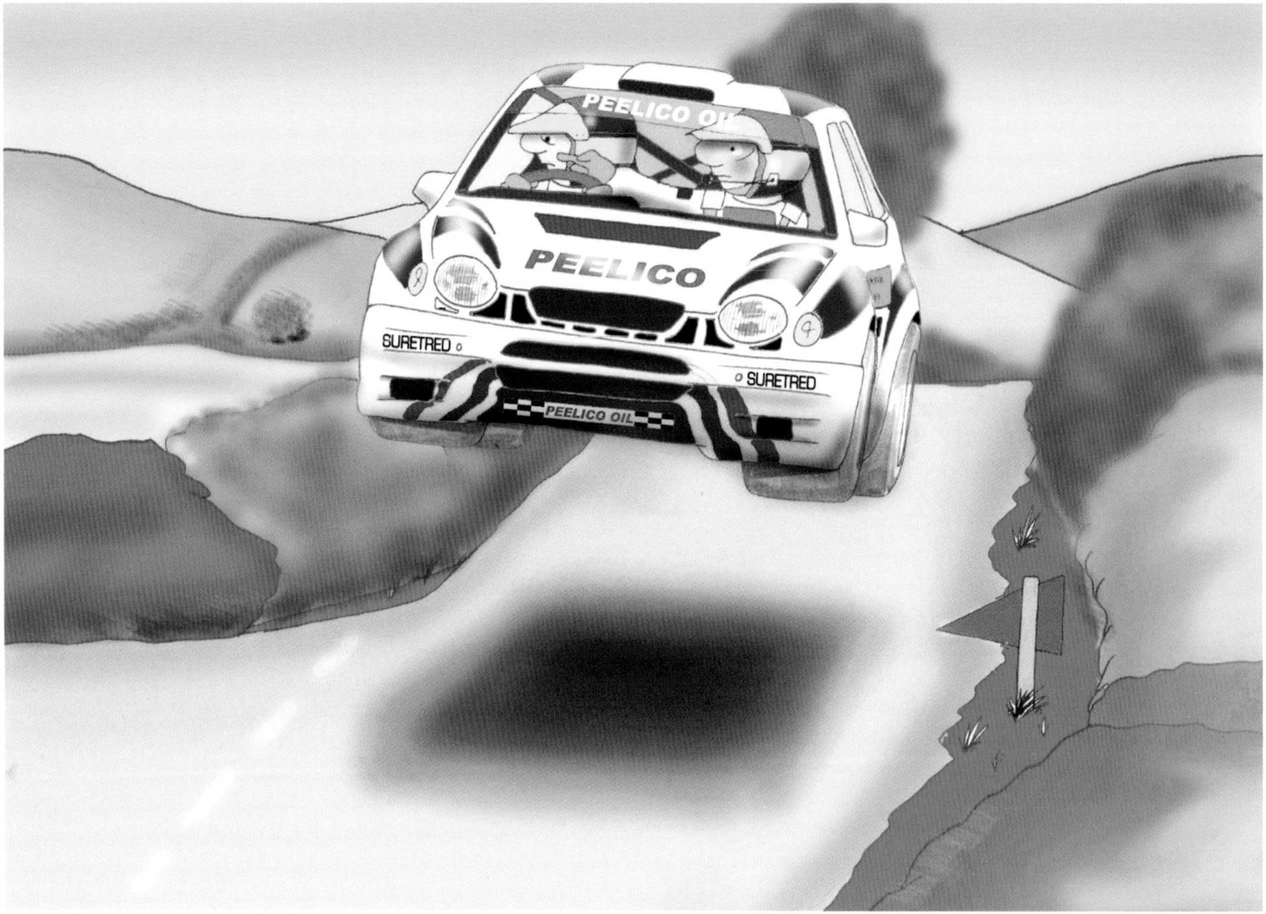
PEELICO OIL
PEELICO
SURETRED
SURETRED
PEELICO OIL

RIGHT!

Paul M Elland

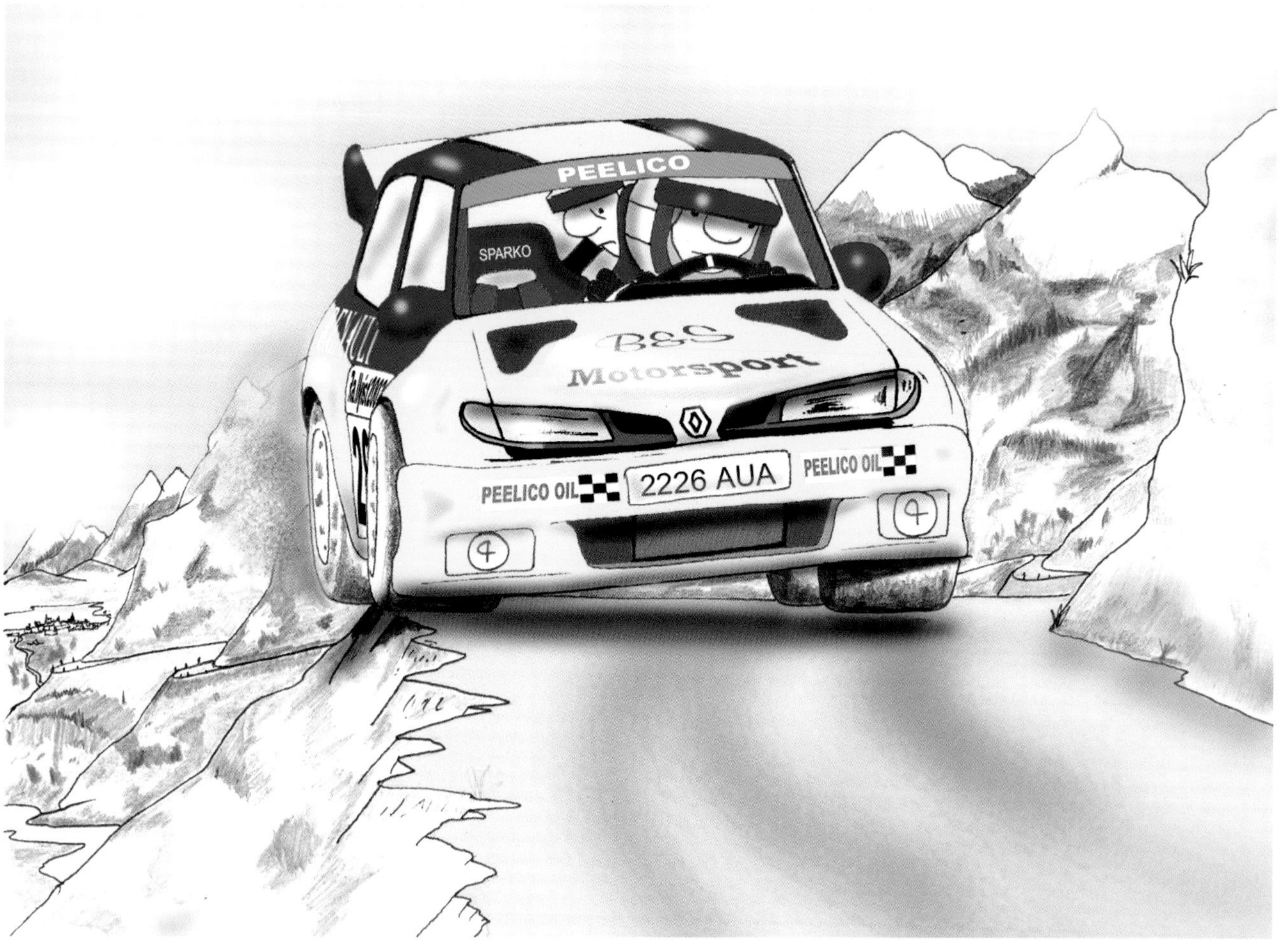
PEELICO
SPARKO
B&S
Motorsport
PEELICO OIL
2226 AUA
PEELICO OIL

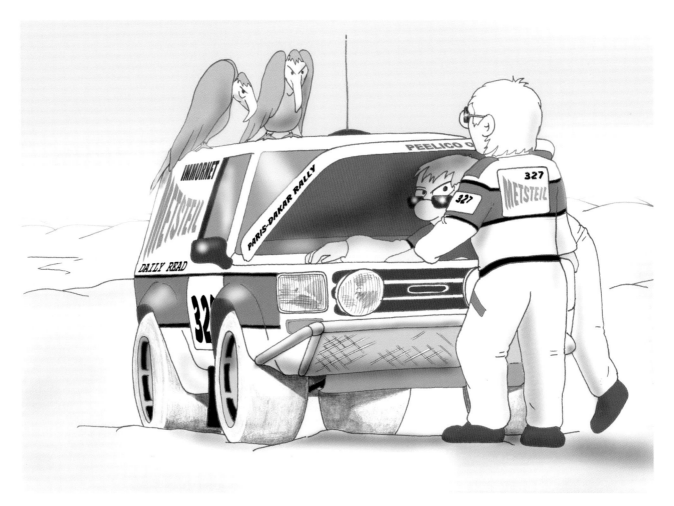

Have a bit of faith, I said I'll get it going.
and I'll get it going

Got a bit carried away
With the Sun Strip

Its worse than we thought,
We forgot to bring the Crisps!

You know we haven't seen that Motorbike
for a while.

I tell you there is no
mention of it in the Road Book!

50

Ah! Remember when spent all day
standing in the snow, and mud, and cold?

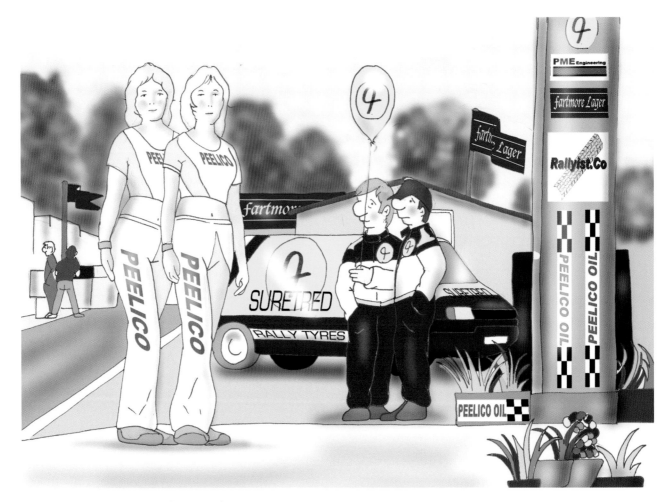

Why do we never get sponsors
like that?

Well baring any silly mistakes
we've got this one in the bag!

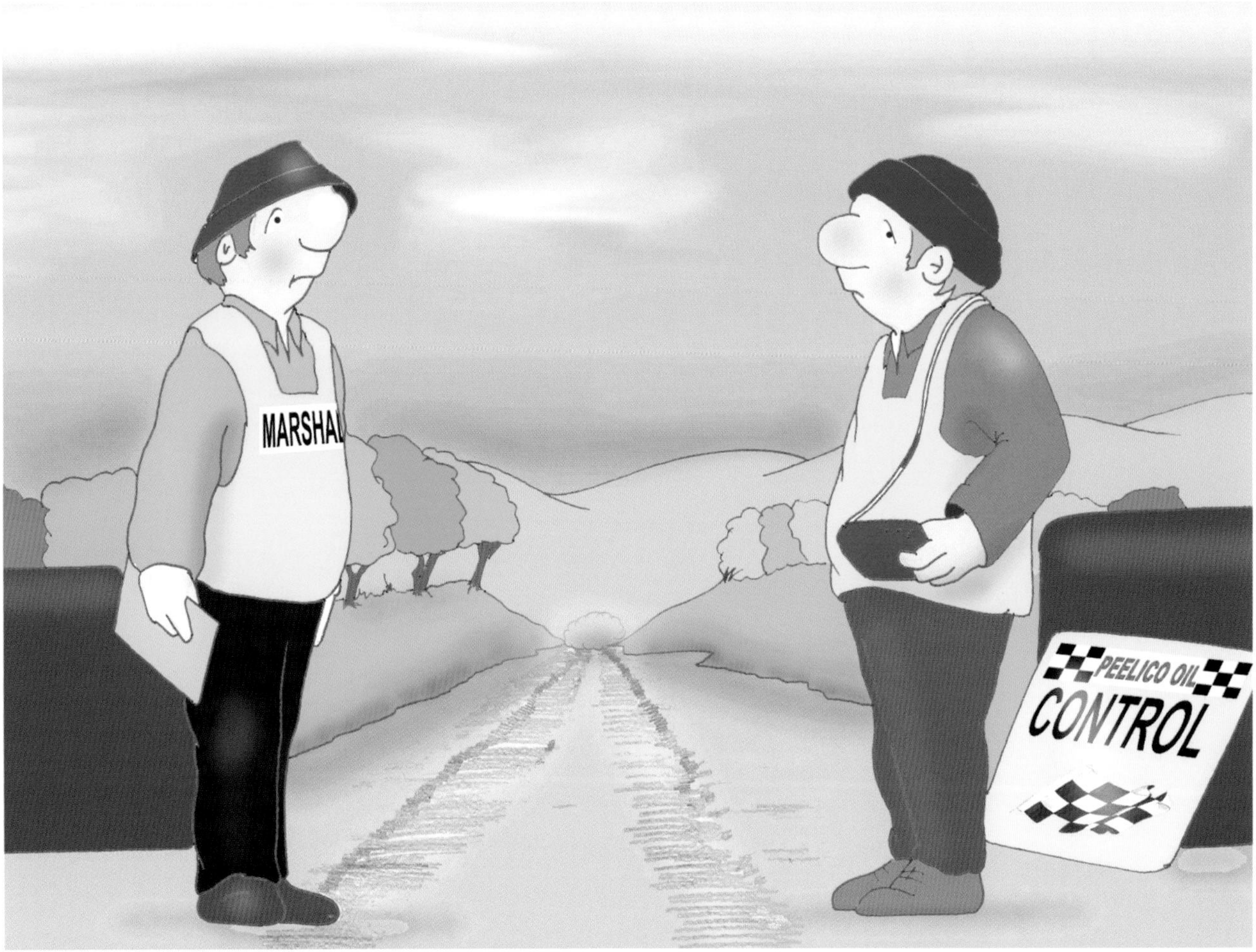
MARSHAL
PEELICO OIL
CONTROL

He Said Thankyou

Paul M Ellerd

Other Titles From Paul M. Ellender.

The Rallyist
The Rallyist-2

Watch out for more great Titles in the future from

Rallyist Publications

And what's coming next?

Rallyist-2

Even More Rallying Exploits
From the Cartoon World of Paul M. Ellender

Another great book from Rallyist Publications Out Mid 2009
Make sure you get a copy.